sangria

FUN AND FESTIVE RECIPES

Mittie Hellmich

Photographs by Victoria Pearson

CHRONICLE BOOKS

SAN FRANCISCO

Text copyright © 2004 by Chronicle Books LLC
Photographs copyright © 2004 by Victoria Pearson

Library of Congress Cataloging-in-Publication Data:
Hellmich, Mittie, 1960–
   Sangria : fun and festive recipes / by Mittie Hellmich ;
photographs by Victoria Pearson.
      p. cm.
   ISBN 0-8118-4290-8 (hardcover)
   1. Cocktails. I. Title.
   TX951.H4523 2004
   641.8'74--dc22
                         2003015017

Manufactured in China.
Design and typesetting by Carole Goodman,
   Blue Anchor Design
Photographer's assistant: Jon Nakano
Prop stylist: Yolande Yorke-Edgell
Prop stylist's assistant: Nori Hubbs
Food stylist: Rori Trovato
Food stylist's assistant: Tina Wilson

Distributed in Canada by Raincoast Books
9050 Shaughnessy Street
Vancouver, British Columbia V6P 6E5

10 9 8 7 6 5 4 3 2 1

Chronicle Books LLC
85 Second Street
San Francisco, California 94105

www.chroniclebooks.com

DEDICATION

This book is dedicated to my sister Nicole Hudson and my brother-in-law Geoff, the perfect traveling companions, whose adventurous spirit made meandering through Spain a rich and memorable experience.

ACKNOWLEDGMENTS

Amid the mountains of succulent fruit and a cellar full of Spanish wine, all in eager anticipation of becoming frosty pitchers of sangrias, I was fortunate enough to have an abundant infusion of assistance from very talented and sangria-savvy people, without which this book could not have been completed.

First and foremost, to my editors at Chronicle Books: a huge thanks to Leslie Jonath, whose conceptually brilliant vision and enthusiasm for this project were pure inspiration; to Bill LeBlond, editor extraordinaire, for his wisdom and support; the sharp and savvy assistant editor Laurel Mainard; and copy editor Sharilyn Hovind. Thanks also to the rest of the Chronicle Books team: designers Pamela Geismar and Carole Goodman and photographer Victoria Pearson.

Many thanks to friends and family, who generously contributed their time, suggestions, and support, and who were more than willing to fearlessly lend their discerning palates to the cause. Nicole Hudson and Geoff Rhoads, Karen Von Clezie and Scott Bartley for hosting tapas- and sangria-testing soirees, as well as contributing their extensive culinary vision. Thanks to Taylor James Pierce, Masha Turchinsky, and Eduardo Gustamante, knowledgeable in all things Spanish, for sharing their wealth of Iberian experiences and insights into the Spanish culture, culinary and otherwise. Thanks to Bryan and Shannon Rhoads, Amanda Rhoads, Alison and Mark Nightingale, Janet Keating and Steven Corson, Dirk and Lisa Pierce, Nick Pierce and Donna Peterson, Bobbie Rhoads and John Magee, who helpfully offered input on the seemingly endless pitchers of sangrias and taste-tested tapas for cultural authenticity. To my nephew and budding writer, Trevor Rhoads, for his fresh editing insights, and nephew Hugo for his overwhelming enthusiasm when it came to tapas-testing.

TABLE OF CONTENTS

INTRODUCTION: VIVA LA SANGRÍA

ANCIENT OLIVE TREES OFFERING A CANOPY OF SHADE FOR AN AFTER-
noon siesta, evenings at the local tapas bar spent deep in conversation, and
refreshing sips of chilled sangria made with seasonal fruits and local wines—
these are quintessential pleasures of the Iberian lifestyle.

Enjoying a wealth of multicultural influences that date back to ancient
times, Spain is a country steeped in rich traditions. The classic sangria beverage itself is centuries old, and the infusion of wine with succulent fruits reflects
Spain's culinary diversity, emphasis on social ritual, and regional produce.
Wine cultivation and trade were conducted by the Phoenicians as far back as
the eighth century B.C., and the first recorded sangria can be traced to the
Romans residing in Andalusia around 300 B.C., who quenched their summer
thirst with a chilled wine beverage infused with fruits.

The practice of steeping fruits in wine sprang from a need to add flavor to
a village's young, light table red that was not particularly robust. Different grapes
were grown in each wine region for local consumption, and the addition of
favorite locally grown fruits and spices resulted in rich, regional variations on
the sangria theme.

Although the concept of the drink has existed since ancient times, the
word *sangría* itself didn't show up until the eighteenth century. Some lexicog-
raphers believe it derives from Sanskrit through the Urdu *sakkari,* meaning
"sugared wine." The more universal and popular belief is that it derives from
sangre, the Spanish word for "blood," referring to the red hue of wine that was
ritualistically imbibed as a sacred beverage.

The Spaniards have an attitude about their wine that logically extends
to sangria: they do not consider wine a product, but simply an elaboration
on something that already exists in nature. The key character of sangria is in its
adventuresome flexibility, enabling endless ingredient variations depending
on the seasonal fruit and the mixologist's preferences. Traditionally made
with light, red wine, bodaciously juicy from hours of soaking up succulent
fruits, it has a balance of flavor from the essential tartness of citrus juxtaposed
with the sweetness of pineapple, peaches, nectarines, berries, apples, pears,
or melon. From there, variations typically include brandy, orange liqueur, or
another flavored liqueur for warmth and fortification, and a refreshing splash
of effervescence from sparkling water. There are now many versions that

have embraced the summery lightness of white and sparkling wines to be used in place of the classic red wine.

Found mostly along the Spanish Mediterranean coastline around Barcelona, sangria today is frequently served to tourists seeking authentic traditional culinary experiences. That is not to say that it has disappeared from other regions—sangria is made with local wines and included in the fabric of daily life in many parts of Spain. Whether it be an outdoor table celebration with friends and neighbors, an afternoon picnic, or part of the social scene at one of the many wine bars, enjoying tapas and sharing a fruity chilled sangria remain a firmly established ritual the Spanish hold dear: good food, good wine, and the opportunity for gathering with friends for pleasurable conversation.

This book explores all aspects of the rich sangria tradition, its ingredients, and its methodology, along with several classic accoutrements of spicy tapas. Here you will find Spanish regional favorites alongside innovative global concoctions, with discussions on various ingredients and the appropriate wines to use. Liquid excursions into Mediterranean coastal sangrias reflect an abundance of peaches, apricots, melons, cherries, grapes, oranges, and pears from Barcelona and Valencia infusing the wonderful sparkling Cavas of Catalonia and light red Riojas. Moorish-influenced southern Andalusian sangrias blend sherry, saffron, figs, and dates with a crisp, dry white wine, sweet Muscat, or red from Valdepeñas. Some exotic concoctions use ingredients that reach beyond Spanish borders.

Ahh, if only we could all adopt the congenial Spanish lifestyle—quality living at a leisurely pace, with pleasant social breaks, fruity chilled sangrias, and delicious tapas. Begin with a summer afternoon garden party or weekend get-together and let *Sangria: Fun and Festive Recipes* be your ticket to Iberian-style bliss. Enjoy!

SANGRIA 101: ON YOUR WAY TO PITCHER PERFECTION

VERSATILITY IS PART OF SANGRIA'S CHARM, SO CONSIDER THIS BOOK YOUR invitation to explore beyond the classic formula and discover innumerable delicious combinations of wine and fruit, whether you are utilizing the recipes offered here or concocting your own. Either way, here are a few basics that can guide you through the sangria methodology, including traditional ways for interchanging ingredients.

Numerous variations exist: To the basic mixture of red wine with fresh citrus slices, brandy is usually added for warmth and fortification, and sparkling water for effervescence and to decrease alcohol content. Other possible additions include various fresh fruits, orange liqueur, sugar for more sweetness, or lemon-lime soda or ginger ale in place of the sparkling water. The sparkling water is sometimes omitted altogether.

FROM THE VINE TO THE WINE TO THE PITCHER

Sangrias have evolved beyond the original motivation behind them—of enhancing cheap local table wines with fruit—to recipes that now call for good-quality, moderately priced wines. Luckily, Spain makes excellent wines at bargain prices, so take advantage and go with the authentic goods (and by all means save your more expensive wines for sipping straight).

In-depth wine information with specific suggestions for each type of wine is given in the recipe sections of this book, but here are the basics: For authenticity, look for a Spanish red Rioja. Sangrias are traditionally made with a juicy, light red wine such as a Rioja Cosecha, or a medium-bodied dry wine, such as a Rioja Reserva. Otherwise, choose a dry, crisp white, brut sparkling wine, or fruity rosé made from the garnacha grape.

Due to their lightness and delicate flavors, white wine, rosés, and sparkling wines are easily interchangeable in any given recipe. Muscat wines are a nice choice for those who prefer a sweeter white wine sangria. Red wine–based sangrias are distinctively more robust, but you can try different varieties, from a Rioja to a Beaujolais to a Bordeaux. There are no hard-and-fast rules here—simply take your favorite sangria recipe and use the wine of your choice. You will discover the truly versatile nature of sangria.

FRUITOLOGY

Sangria, by definition, is fruit-infused wine, so the abundance of fruity possibilities really comes down to a question of preference. A good place to start is with your favorite local fruits. The recipes in this book call for fruits that are easily accessible in one form or another—whether fresh, frozen, juice, or nectar. Fortunately, supermarkets and specialty grocers are steadily improving at stocking a wide variety of exotic fruits.

Rules of thumb:

- Look for unblemished fruits that are ripe or close to ripe.

- Never refrigerate unripe fruit.

- Wash fruit just prior to using. If the fruit is frozen, rinse it.

Opinions differ on the amount of time the fruit should be left to macerate in the wine: some suggest adding it shortly before drinking to preserve the flavor, but the prevailing opinion is to let the fruit infuse the wine for at least a few hours.

Succulent, ripe fruit or freshly squeezed juice will always give the best flavor, of course, but when a fruit is out of season, frozen whole fruit is a fine substitution. It may be added to the wine when still slightly frozen, as it will thaw while macerating. If you are in a real pinch and a particular fresh or frozen fruit is not available, canned or jarred fruit strained from its juice is an option. It needs minimal maceration time in the wine and should be added shortly before serving the sangria.

Straining Fruits from Sangria
Straining sangria? Why, that's blasphemy! There are only a few occasions when you will need to strain the fruit from the wine after the maceration process, once the flavors have mingled. Again, it all comes down to a question of personal preference. For those who are bothered by little fig seeds or floating lavender, straining is an option. Of course, if you are planning to transfer your sangria into a bota bag (traveling wine pouch), straining is a necessity.

Citrus
Considering that many sangria recipes use citrus fruits, here are a few things to keep in mind:

• Choose unblemished fruits and wash before preparing.

• After slicing a fruit, carefully seed the slices.

When cutting zest, avoid as much of the bitter white pith as possible. Grate the shiny, outer peel of the citrus fruit with a fine grater or a zester (a sharp metal tool with a row of tiny holes at the end).

Fruit Juices
Just about any fruit juice is a welcome ingredient, from the traditional splash of orange juice to more exotic tropical juices such as guava or papaya. Just how much fruity flavor you choose to add in respect to the wine is purely a personal preference.

Brandies and Liqueurs
Brandy is the traditional ingredient used to fortify sangria, typically a young, inexpensive variety, but you can try Chilean Pisco brandy for an added bite. Some variations contain fruit-flavored brandy, orange liqueur, cognac, plain or flavored vodka, or rum for additional flavor complexity. Orange liqueurs are easily interchangeable and you can substitute Cointreau or Grand Marnier for

the usual Triple Sec. Basically, 4 to 5 ounces of any fruit- or herb-based liqueur is an appropriate addition.

SPARKLING WATERS AND SODAS

Variations include a splash of club soda, lemonade, ginger ale, or a sparkling fruit beverage such as grapefruit, orange, or lemon-lime. Add to sangria right before serving to preserve the effervescence and stir with a wooden or plastic (not metal) spoon.

CHILL FACTORS

First and foremost, wines should be thoroughly chilled before you add them to the other sangria ingredients. This is especially important if you are planning to blend and serve the sangria right away. Chill fruit juices, sparkling beverages, and other liquid ingredients as well. (There is no need to chill brandy or liqueurs.)

Chill times for sangrias vary, depending on which ingredients you are using. For example, fresh fruit mixed with white, red, rosé, or Muscat wine can be chilled overnight (or for up to 24 hours, for the best flavor results). Sangria is a natural choice for entertaining, as you can always be prepared with pitchers chilling overnight for the next day's festivities.

Sangrias made with sparkling wine, on the other hand, need a slightly different approach. The fruit and other ingredients need to be chilled for only a few hours at most before the sparkling wine is added, as they have minimal liquid in which to macerate. Add the chilled sparkling wine to the fruit mixture right before serving to preserve the effervescence.

Ice versus No Ice

Where ice is concerned, you and your guests may prefer your sangria as is—refreshingly chilled—or on the rocks, a little colder (albeit slightly diluted once the ice starts melting). Offer ice cubes for glasses, but do not put them in your pitcher or punch bowl. Sangrias made with sparkling wine are often enjoyed without ice.

TO GARNISH OR NOT TO GARNISH

When it comes to sangrias, garnishes aren't absolutely necessary, given the beautiful display of fruits that will be floating in your glass, but if you feel the need, by all means get extroverted with your garnishing and revel in lush ornamentation. Whichever aesthetic path you choose to follow—be it a single floating rose petal or an elaborate shish kebab of fresh fruits—garnishes will ornament your drinks with style. You can garnish the pitcher or punch bowl, or individual glasses.

Edible Flowers

Edible flowers—such as violets, borage, rose petals, orange blossoms, and hibiscus—add an elegant touch to sangrias.

Choose pesticide-free blooms.

Gently rinse the flower or petals and float on the top of the cocktail, or skewer flower blossoms with a pick and set on the rim.

MULTIPLYING FOR A PARTY

The sangria recipes in this book have been formulated to serve about four people per 750ml bottle of wine. If you wish to accommodate a slightly larger group, there is a certain amount of flexibility the infused fruit flavor will allow: you can add an additional half bottle of wine or more club soda or fruit juice to extend the sangria. Beyond that, simply double or triple the recipe (and use a larger pitcher or a few pitchers) for groups of eight or more.

My preference when I'm serving a crowd is to follow the traditional sangria party ritual. One of the benefits of this versatile and highly social drink is that you can add to it as your party expands. Start with a two-bottle batch of your favorite sangria in a large punch bowl. As the party progresses, guests arrive, bringing a fruit and/or a bottle of wine (you can let them know ahead of time what type of wine) that can be added to the bowl as the sangria gets depleted. Keep a few bottles of sparkling wine and club soda on hand for a bit of effervescence. As to the fruit, you can cut up large amounts of ripe fruit ahead of time and refrigerate or freeze for use at the party.

Note: It is important to note that sangrias, although mild and fruity in taste and easy to drink, do contain a fair amount of alcohol. A Spanish-style party is always more pleasant when you and your guests drink sangria in moderation.

SANGRÍA TINTA

RED WINE SANGRIA

LIGHT RED WINES ARE THE BEST PLACE TO BEGIN

when looking to create the quintessential Spanish sangria, specifically a dry, light red Rioja (named after the region in Spain in which it is produced). While using a Rioja will enhance the authenticity of your sangria, you can also try other light reds such as Gamay, Bardolino, Beaujolais, Dolcetto, Freisa, Grignolino, or Lambrusco. If you prefer, feel free to venture into the territory of more robust red wines such as Merlot, Burgundy, Zinfandel, or Pinot Noir. (Cabernet Franc and Cabernet Sauvignon are too heavy for this drink.)

For a pleasurable adventure for the palate, enjoy your red wine sangria with a prosciutto or other cured ham such as Serrano paired with melon or the Classic Andalusian Gazpacho (page 77). It also nicely complements grilled salmon and pasta dishes.

This chapter begins with the classic sangria formula in all its traditional glory, then expands upon it to include variations that are lush in flavor, from the exotic and abundantly fruity to the innovative and sublimely subtle.

Classic Spanish Sangria

Spanish sangria began simply as a blend of fresh orange juice and a light red wine, mixed with a little sugar and lemon juice and served as a chilled punch. (The ancient Romans were also known to enjoy their wine with a float of olive oil, a culinary innovation we will choose to ignore for this book.) From there it evolved into this classic recipe, complete with fresh slices of citrus fruit, brandy for warmth and depth, and the effervescence of club soda. Variations have been known to include slices of apples, Cointreau in place of the brandy, and ginger ale or even grapefruit soda for the fizz factor. This is the quintessential recipe: tried and true, and therefore delicious.

1 orange, sliced	2 tablespoons sugar
1 lime, sliced	750ml bottle light red wine, chilled
½ lemon, sliced	12 ounces club soda, chilled
1½ ounces brandy	About 3 cups ice cubes

In a large (at least 2-quart) glass pitcher, combine the orange, lime, and lemon slices. Add the brandy and sugar, and stir until the sugar has dissolved. Slowly pour in the wine, stirring gently. Refrigerate for at least 2 hours or as long as overnight.

When ready to serve, add the club soda and stir gently with a long-handled wooden spoon. Fill highballs, wineglasses, or other decorative glasses with ice cubes and slowly pour the sangria over the ice, allowing fruit slices to fall into the glasses.

SERVES 4 TO 6

Fig, Cherry, and Cognac Sangria

Voluptuous and elegant, this sangria boasts intense flavors of cherry and fig (compliments of the Moorish influence on Spanish cuisine) through the fruity depth of the wine, with the added warmth of cognac. Served without the club soda, it becomes a perfect after-dinner sipping treat, fabulous with a bit of blue cheese such as a Spanish Cabrales or Gamonedo, or a British Stilton—and, definitely, chocolate.

4 fresh or dried figs, sliced

1 cup dried pitted cherries

2 ounces cognac

2 tablespoons honey, warmed

750ml bottle light red wine, chilled

12 ounces club soda, chilled (optional)

About 3 cups ice cubes

4 to 6 mint sprigs for garnish (optional)

In a large (at least 2-quart) glass container, combine the figs and cherries. Add the cognac and honey, and stir until the honey has dissolved. Slowly pour in the wine, stirring gently. Refrigerate for at least 2 hours or as long as overnight.

When ready to serve, strain through a fine-mesh sieve into a glass pitcher. Add the club soda, if using, and stir gently with a long-handled wooden spoon. Fill highballs, wineglasses, or other decorative glasses with ice cubes and pour the sangria over the ice. Garnish each glass with a mint sprig, if desired.

SERVES 4 TO 6

Sparkling Apple Cider Sangria

This is a light and thoroughly pleasant sangria full of puckery apple flavor with the snappy fizz of sparkling apple cider. A few strips of lemon and orange peel add a zesty accent. Use either Fuji apples, for sweet subtlety, or Granny Smiths, for extra tartness. Perfect for those early fall days still clinging to the warmth of summer.

2 apples, cored and sliced

2 ounces Calvados

2 long strips lemon peel, plus
  3 to 4 shorter strips for garnish

2 long strips orange peel, plus
  3 to 4 shorter strips for garnish

Pinch of ground cinnamon

750ml bottle light red wine, chilled

750ml bottle sparkling nonalcoholic
  apple cider, chilled

About 4 cups ice cubes

In a large (at least 2-quart) glass pitcher, combine the apple slices, Calvados, long citrus peels, and cinnamon. Slowly pour in the wine, stirring gently. Refrigerate for at least 2 hours or as long as overnight.

When ready to serve, add the sparkling apple cider and stir gently with a long-handled wooden spoon. Fill highballs, wineglasses, or other decorative glasses with ice cubes and slowly pour the sangria over the ice, allowing apple slices to fall into the glasses. Garnish each glass with a strip of lemon or orange peel.

SERVES 6 TO 8

Mango Cointreau Sangria

The intriguing juxtaposition of red wine with sweet, fragrant mango and tangy citrus evokes a sun- and bliss-filled holiday on some far-off island south of the equator. The best mangos will have orange-red tones and are ripe when slightly soft to the touch when gently squeezed.

2 ripe mangos, peeled, pitted, and sliced

1 orange, sliced

½ lime, sliced

½ lemon, sliced

2 ounces Cointreau

750ml bottle light red wine, chilled

6 ounces club soda, chilled

About 3 cups ice cubes

In a large (at least 2-quart) glass pitcher, mix together the mango, orange, lime, and lemon slices. Add the Cointreau and stir to combine. Slowly pour in the wine, stirring gently. Refrigerate for at least 2 hours or as long as overnight.

When ready to serve, add the club soda and stir gently with a long-handled wooden spoon. Fill highballs, wineglasses, or other decorative glasses with ice cubes and slowly pour the sangria over the ice, allowing fruit slices to fall into the glasses.

SERVES 4 TO 6

Spanish Harlem Sangria

This pitcher of spiced-up sangria evokes all the festive allure of a street fair in Spanish Harlem. Like a great salsa beat, red bell pepper hits the perfect zesty note, while a splash of Chilean Pisco brandy, made from muscat grapes, rounds out the medley of flavors with an aromatic and warm finish.

1 orange, sliced

1 apple, cored and sliced

¼ cup diced red bell pepper

2 ounces Pisco brandy

750ml bottle light red wine, chilled

12 ounces club soda, chilled

About 3 cups ice cubes

In a large (at least 2-quart) glass pitcher, combine the orange and apple slices, bell pepper, and brandy. Slowly pour in the wine, stirring gently. Refrigerate for at least 2 hours or as long as overnight.

When ready to serve, add the club soda and stir gently with a long-handled wooden spoon. Fill highballs, wineglasses, or other decorative glasses with ice cubes and slowly pour the sangria over the ice, allowing fruit slices and bell pepper pieces to fall into the glasses.

SERVES 4 TO 6

Variation: To bring a refreshing summery note to the mix of flavors, add 1 cup seeded and cubed watermelon.

Persimmon, Pomegranate, and Tangerine Sangria

Creating a pitcher of Dionysian enchantment, an opulent combination of exotic fruit flavors infuses this sangria: juicy, sweet-tart pomegranate, delicately sweet persimmon, and tangy tangerine.

2 persimmons, peeled, seeded, and quartered (see note)

Seeds from 1 pomegranate (see note)

2 tangerines, sliced

2 ounces Mandarine Napoleon liqueur or other orange liqueur

750ml bottle light red wine, chilled

12 ounces club soda, chilled

About 3 cups ice cubes

In a large (at least 2-quart) glass pitcher, mix together the persimmon pulp, pomegranate seeds, and tangerine slices. Add the liqueur and stir to combine. Slowly pour in the wine, stirring gently. Refrigerate for at least 2 hours or as long as overnight.

When ready to serve, add the club soda and stir gently with a long-handled wooden spoon. Fill highballs, wineglasses, or other decorative glasses with ice cubes and slowly pour the sangria over the ice, allowing fruit pieces to fall into the glasses.

Note: Look for red-orange Hachiya persimmons that are soft, with jelly-like pulp and slightly browned skin when ripe or the firmer, orange Fuyu variety. Pomegranates have smooth leathery skin with a brownish yellow to red color and a multitude of tiny seeds inside, each surrounded by a transparent red juicy pulp.

SERVES 4 TO 6

Ginger Pear Sangria

Pan-Asian and Spanish sensibilities meld seamlessly in this delightful sangria. A subtle hint of spicy ginger permeates and infuses this pear-nectared wine, which is complete with the smoothness of pear brandy and the zing of orange zest.

2 ripe pears, cored and sliced

¼ cup peeled and thinly sliced fresh ginger

2 tablespoons orange zest

1 ounce pear brandy

750ml bottle light red wine, chilled

6 ounces club soda, chilled

About 3 cups ice cubes

In a large (at least 2-quart) glass pitcher, mix together the pear and ginger slices and orange zest. Add the pear brandy and stir to combine. Slowly pour in the wine, stirring gently. Refrigerate for at least 2 hours or as long as overnight.

When ready to serve, add the club soda and stir gently with a long-handled wooden spoon. Fill highballs, wineglasses, or other decorative glasses with ice cubes and slowly pour the sangria over the ice, allowing pear slices to fall into the glasses.

SERVES 4

Stone Fruit Zurra

In southern Spain, you will come across pitchers of *zurra,* a sangria usually made with peaches or nectarines. Similar in concept is the dessert *zurracapote*— dried apricots and prunes simmered in red wine with cinnamon and lemon peel. This sangria reflects these enchanting elements. A good Bordeaux is an excellent choice for this recipe, guaranteeing a rich sangria experience.

2 peaches, pitted and sliced

2 nectarines, pitted and sliced

1 cup dried apricot slices

2 tablespoons lemon zest

1 teaspoon ground cinnamon

2 ounces apricot brandy

750ml bottle light red wine, chilled

12 ounces club soda, chilled

About 3 cups ice cubes

In a large (at least 2-quart) glass pitcher, mix together the peach, nectarine, and apricot slices, lemon zest, and cinnamon. Add the apricot brandy and stir to combine. Slowly pour in the wine, stirring gently. Refrigerate for at least 2 hours or as long as overnight.

When ready to serve, add the club soda and stir gently with a long-handled wooden spoon. Fill highballs, wineglasses, or other decorative glasses with ice cubes and slowly pour the sangria over the ice, allowing fruit slices to fall into the glasses.

SERVES 4 TO 6

Variation: For an equally luscious, light, and summery version, substitute a white wine such as a Sauvignon Blanc.

La Mancha Sangria

If you and your companions are feeling the need to follow a delusional quest, this is the ideal libation to take with you in a bota bag. La Mancha, Spain, is famous not only for Cervantes's tale of the mad but chivalrous Don Quixote, but also for its saffron, Manchego cheese, and cheap red table wine. This rich sangria is perfumed with the regional flavors of anise (via the liqueurs), lemon, and saffron, with fresh strawberries for fruitiness. For authenticity, use a dry red wine from the La Mancha region—there are a few good ones imported to the United States. To add a festive touch, this sangria is lovely with a splash of sparkling wine in place of the club soda.

2 cups fresh strawberries, hulled and sliced

1 teaspoon saffron threads (about 2 pinches)

2 tablespoons lemon zest

2 ounces Galliano

½ ounce Pernod or Spanish Ojen

750ml bottle light red wine, chilled

12 ounces club soda or sparkling wine, chilled

About 3 cups ice cubes

4 to 6 long strips lemon peel for garnish (optional)

In a large (at least 2-quart) glass pitcher, mix together the strawberries, saffron, and lemon zest. Add the Galliano and Pernod or Ojen, and stir to combine. Slowly pour in the wine, stirring gently. Refrigerate for at least 2 hours or as long as overnight.

When ready to serve, slowly add the club soda or sparkling wine and stir gently with a long-handled wooden spoon. Fill highballs, wineglasses, or other decorative glasses with ice cubes and slowly pour the sangria over the ice, allowing strawberry slices to fall into the glasses.

Garnish each glass with a slice of lemon peel, if desired.

SERVES 4 TO 6 DELUSIONAL OPTIMISTS

Gaudíesque Sangria

This elaborate sangria is a nod to the great city of Barcelona and to the architectural aesthetics of Antonio Gaudí, Barcelona's famed and beloved architect. It celebrates the abundant fruits of the Catalonia region, while reflecting Gaudí's genius for balancing a multitude of fantastic architectural embellishments. Over the top is where it's at! Delectable and multilayered, the sangria has a whisper of nuttiness from Frangelico, a rich hazelnut liqueur, and is fittingly topped with Cava, the sparkling wine produced in this area of Spain.

1 peach, pitted and sliced

2 apricots, pitted and sliced

1 pear, cored and sliced

1 cup fresh or canned cherries, pitted

1 cup seeded and cubed honeydew melon

2 ounces Frangelico

750ml bottle light red wine, chilled

750ml bottle brut Cava or other sparkling wine, chilled

About 3 cups ice cubes (optional)

In a large (at least 2-quart) glass pitcher, mix together the fruit pieces. Add the Frangelico and stir to combine. Slowly pour in the red wine, stirring gently. Refrigerate for at least 2 hours or as long as overnight.

When ready to serve, slowly add the sparkling wine, stirring gently with a long-handled wooden spoon. Fill champagne flutes, wineglasses, or other decorative glasses with ice cubes, if using, and slowly pour the sangria over the ice, allowing fruit pieces to fall into the glasses.

SERVES 6 TO 8

Limonada España

A traditional libation in Spain, *limonada* usually consists of water, lemon juice, lemon quarters, red wine, sugar, and cubed peaches. I have elaborated on it slightly by adding one of Spain's favorite liqueurs, Licor 43. Produced and blended according to a recipe dating back to 200 B.C., this complex liqueur contains 43 fruits and herbal elements, and imparts a strong vanilla flavor that adds a lovely dimension to this spunky sangria.

2 lemons, sliced

2 peaches, pitted and sliced

½ cup fresh lemon juice

3 ounces Licor 43

¼ cup sugar

750ml bottle light red wine, chilled

12 ounces club soda, chilled

About 3 cups ice cubes

In a large (at least 2-quart) glass pitcher, combine the lemon and peach slices. Add the lemon juice, Licor 43, and sugar and stir until the sugar has dissolved. Slowly pour in the wine, stirring gently. Refrigerate for at least 2 hours or as long as overnight.

When ready to serve, add the club soda and stir gently with a long-handled wooden spoon. Fill highballs, wineglasses, or other decorative glasses with ice cubes and slowly pour the sangria over the ice, allowing fruit slices to fall into the glasses.

SERVES 4 TO 6

SANGRÍA BLANCA
WHITE WINE SANGRIA

WHITE WINE SANGRIAS ARE NOT AS STEEPED IN TRADITION as those made with red wine, nor are they as common—which only adds to their allure. These sangrias are a delightful departure, breezy light and summery, and much more versatile. They allow the subtleties of a wide variety of fruits to come through more clearly, letting the flavors really sing out. A good Spanish white Rioja is the ideal wine to use, but any crisp, relatively dry white wine will do fine, such as a Bordeaux Blanc, Pinot Gris (or Pinot Grigio), or Sauvignon Blanc.

Serve your white wine sangria with grilled chicken, fish, shellfish, or vegetables. Try Grilled Garlic Shrimp with Saffron (page 71) or the Grilled Asparagus with Almonds (page 72).

Blood Orange and Campari Sangria

A ruby-hued sangria with herbal tones, this unique mixture is as beautiful as it is delicious, and is a visual metaphor to the classic sangria, translated via white wine. The sweetness of ruby-red blood oranges counterbalances the bitter-sweetness of Campari, making this the quintessential Italian summer aperitif.

2 blood oranges, sliced	750ml bottle dry white wine, chilled
2 ounces Campari	12 ounces club soda, chilled
2 tablespoons sugar	About 3 cups ice cubes

In a large (at least 2-quart) glass pitcher, combine the orange slices, Campari, and sugar, and stir until the sugar has dissolved. Slowly pour in the wine, stirring gently. Refrigerate for at least 2 hours or as long as overnight.

When ready to serve, add the club soda and stir gently with a long-handled wooden spoon. Fill highballs, wineglasses, or other decorative glasses with ice cubes and slowly pour the sangria over the ice, allowing orange slices to fall into the glasses.

SERVES 4 TO 6

Strawberry Mint Sangria

For those who are strawberry fans, this is the sangria for you—and as great summertime quenchers go, it just doesn't get any better than this. The sweet flavor of strawberries has a refreshing whisper of mint drifting through it, and the berries suffuse the white wine with a delicate pink hue.

2 cups strawberries, hulled and sliced

½ cup fresh mint leaves (approximately 20 leaves); plus 4 to 6 mint sprigs for garnish (optional)

1½ ounces brandy

750ml bottle dry white wine, chilled

12 ounces club soda, chilled

About 3 cups ice cubes

In a large (at least 2-quart) glass pitcher, combine the strawberries, mint, and brandy. Slowly pour in the wine, stirring gently. Refrigerate for at least 2 hours or as long as overnight. (Remove the mint leaves from the sangria after 2 hours.)

When ready to serve, add the club soda and stir gently with a long-handled wooden spoon. Fill highballs, wineglasses, or other decorative glasses with ice cubes and slowly pour the sangria over the ice, allowing strawberry slices to fall into the glasses. Garnish each glass with a mint sprig, if desired.

SERVES 4 TO 6

Sangri-la

Here the heady, lush flavors of a tropical paradise—a sangria Shangri-la—
converge with crisp, refreshing white wine. Reminiscent of a great piña colada,
this sangria seems infused with sunshine. Fresh coconut meat is preferred for the
freshest flavor, but if it's unavailable, substitute either coconut cream or
coconut milk.

2 cups cubed fresh or frozen pineapple

½ orange, sliced

½ lime, sliced

⅓ cup diced fresh coconut meat,
   or 2 tablespoons coconut cream
   or coconut milk

2 ounces Grand Marnier

750ml bottle dry white wine, chilled

12 ounces club soda, chilled

About 3 cups ice cubes

In a large (at least 2-quart) glass pitcher, mix together the pineapple, orange
and lime slices, and the coconut. Add the Grand Marnier and stir to combine.
Slowly pour in the wine, stirring gently. Refrigerate for at least 2 hours or as
long as overnight.

When ready to serve, add the club soda and stir gently with a long-
handled wooden spoon. Fill highballs, wineglasses, or other decorative glasses
with ice cubes and slowly pour the sangria over the ice, allowing fruit pieces to
fall into the glasses.

SERVES 4 TO 6

Tangerine, Watermelon, and Grapefruit Sangria

The quintessential summer fruit, juicy sweet watermelon makes the perfect liaison between the citrusy tangerine and tart grapefruit. These fruit flavors meld into the perfect brunch-worthy sangria that is drinkable to a fault. If you prefer more citrus flavor, top with a sparkling orange beverage such as Orangina or San Pellegrino Aranciata.

2 cups seeded and cubed watermelon

1 tangerine, sliced

½ grapefruit, sliced

2 ounces Triple Sec or other orange liqueur

750ml bottle dry white wine, chilled

12 ounces club soda or sparkling orange beverage, chilled

About 3 cups ice cubes

In a large (at least 2-quart) glass pitcher, mix together the watermelon and citrus slices. Add the Triple Sec and stir to combine. Slowly pour in the wine, stirring gently. Refrigerate for at least 2 hours or as long as overnight.

When ready to serve, add the club soda or orange beverage and stir gently with a long-handled wooden spoon. Fill highballs, wineglasses, or other decorative glasses with ice cubes and slowly pour the sangria over the ice, allowing fruit pieces to fall into the glasses.

SERVES 4 TO 6

Roman Holiday

Consider this sangria—brimming with the flavors of an Italian summer—a holiday for the palate. It conjures up breezy afternoons relaxing after a day of tooling along the Mediterranean on a Vespa. The fruit flavors are emphasized with the addition of peach brandy and accented with the lemony zing of Lemoncello (also found as Limoncello), a fabulous Italian liqueur. For the wine, Pinot Grigio is an excellent choice for this recipe, and try Prosecco (an Italian sparkling wine) in place of the club soda for the effervescence.

2 ripe peaches, pitted and sliced

1 cup seedless red grapes, halved

1 cup seedless green grapes, halved

2 lemon slices

2 ounces peach brandy

1 ounce Lemoncello or other lemon liqueur

1 tablespoon sugar

750ml bottle dry white wine, chilled

12 ounces club soda or Prosecco, chilled

About 3 cups ice cubes (optional)

In a large (at least 2-quart) glass pitcher, combine the peach slices, grapes, and lemon slices. Add the peach brandy, Lemoncello, and sugar, and stir until the sugar has dissolved. Slowly pour in the white wine, stirring gently. Refrigerate for at least 2 hours or as long as overnight.

When ready to serve, add the club soda or Prosecco and stir gently with a long-handled wooden spoon. Fill highballs, wineglasses, or other decorative glasses with ice cubes, if using, and slowly pour the sangria over the ice, allowing fruit pieces to fall into the glasses.

SERVES 4 TO 6

Ginger Plum Sangria

Influenced by the aromatic ingredients of Japanese cuisine, this sangria is delicately flavored with sweet purple plums, fresh ginger, and the pleasant tang of sake, which together deliver a world-class taste experience. I prefer this sangria with sparkling wine in place of the club soda. Best flavor results are obtained if you use a good-quality sake.

6 fresh, thawed if frozen, or canned purple plums, pitted and sliced

½ cup peeled and thinly sliced fresh ginger

½ cup good-quality sake

1 tablespoon sugar

750ml bottle dry white wine, chilled

12 ounces club soda or sparkling wine, chilled

About 3 cups ice cubes (optional)

8 to 12 orange blossoms or other edible flowers for garnish (optional)

4 to 6 pieces candied ginger for garnish (optional)

In a large (at least 2-quart) glass pitcher, combine the plum slices, ginger, sake, and sugar, and stir until the sugar has dissolved. Slowly pour in the white wine, stirring gently. Refrigerate for at least 2 hours or as long as overnight.

When ready to serve, slowly add the club soda or sparkling wine and stir gently with a long-handled wooden spoon. Fill highballs, wineglasses, or other decorative glasses with ice cubes, if using, and slowly pour the sangria over the ice, allowing plum and ginger slices to fall into the glasses. If desired, float a couple of orange blossoms on top and garnish the rim of each glass with a slice of candied ginger.

SERVES 4 TO 6

Sangria Caliente

A subtle heat envelopes this peach-hued sangria. Hot jalapeño pepper, tart green apple, and succulently sweet plum, apricot, and peach are spiked with a fiery shot of tequila to give it an extra south-of-the-border kick. The longer it sits, the hotter it gets (you can remove the pepper slices once the heat is to your liking).

1 Granny Smith apple, cored and sliced

1 peach, pitted and sliced

1 plum, pitted and sliced

1 apricot, pitted and sliced

3 thin slices fresh or pickled jalapeño pepper, or to taste

2 ounces tequila

2 tablespoons sugar

750ml bottle dry white wine, chilled

12 ounces club soda, chilled

About 3 cups ice cubes

In a large (at least 2-quart) glass pitcher, combine the fruit and jalapeño slices, tequila, and sugar, and stir until the sugar has dissolved. Slowly pour in the wine, stirring gently. Refrigerate for at least 2 hours or as long as overnight.

When ready to serve, add the club soda and stir gently with a long-handled wooden spoon. Fill highballs, wineglasses, or other decorative glasses with ice cubes and slowly pour the sangria over the ice, allowing fruit pieces (but not pepper slices!) to fall into the glasses.

SERVES 4 TO 6

Summer Melon Sangria

A trio of melons infuses this warm-weather sangria cooler with sweet, summery flavor, while lemon, lime, and Grand Marnier add citrusy zest. To really push the melon factor over the edge, a few ounces of Midori—a chartreuse muskmelon liqueur—will oblige.

1 cup seeded and cubed watermelon

1 cup seeded and cubed honeydew melon

1 cup seeded and cubed cantaloupe

2 lemon slices

1 lime slice

1 ounce Grand Marnier

2 ounces Midori

750ml bottle dry white wine, chilled

12 ounces club soda, chilled

About 3 cups ice cubes

In a large (at least 2-quart) glass pitcher, mix together the melon cubes and lemon and lime slices. Add the Grand Marnier and Midori, and stir to combine. Slowly pour in the wine, stirring gently. Refrigerate for at least 2 hours or as long as overnight.

When ready to serve, add the club soda and stir gently with a long-handled wooden spoon. Fill highballs, wineglasses, or other decorative glasses with ice cubes and slowly pour the sangria over the ice, allowing melon cubes and citrus slices to fall into the glasses.

SERVES 4 TO 6

Mango Lemongrass Sangria

Suffusing this exotic sangria with fragrant Asian flavor, the delicate lemony tones of lemongrass are wonderfully paired with the intense sweetness of mango and accented with the almond whisper of amaretto liqueur. Serve with grilled fish and dishes such as Grilled Garlic Shrimp with Saffron (page 71).

2 ripe mangos, peeled, seeded, and sliced

2 lemongrass stalks—tender midsection only—cut into 2-inch pieces

1½ ounces amaretto

750ml bottle dry white wine, chilled

12 ounces club soda, chilled

About 3 cups ice cubes

In a large (at least 2-quart) glass pitcher, mix together the mango slices and lemongrass. Add the amaretto and stir to combine. Slowly pour in the wine, stirring gently. Refrigerate for at least 2 hours or as long as overnight.

When ready to serve, add the club soda and stir gently with a long-handled wooden spoon. Fill highballs, wineglasses, or other decorative glasses with ice cubes and slowly pour the sangria over the ice, allowing mango slices (but not lemongrass) to fall into the glasses.

SERVES 4 TO 6

Aquavit and Berry Sangria

When you mingle the flavors of dark, juicy berries with fresh mint and citrus, you have the elemental taste of pure summer, and especially so if ingredients are picked fresh from the garden. Conjured up for the celebration of a friend's summer wedding, this is luscious and beautiful served in huge frosty pitchers. Fresh berries are best, but frozen are fine in a pinch (as well as canned, if you must—the berry syrup actually adds an extra bit of sweetness). Similar to a schnapps, Scandinavian aquavit is flavored with fragrant spices such as caraway, aniseed, or bitter orange, and adds a fortified kick to this berry brew. If you can't find it, substitute an orange- or currant-flavored vodka.

2 cups fresh or frozen blackberries, rinsed

1 cup fresh or frozen boysenberries, rinsed

1 lemon, sliced

½ grapefruit, sliced

¼ cup fresh mint leaves (approximately 10 leaves)

2 ounces orange flavored aquavit (see headnote)

2 ounces Chambord

750ml bottle dry white wine, chilled

750ml bottle sparkling wine, chilled

In a large (at least 2-quart) glass pitcher, mix together the berries, citrus slices, and mint. Add the aquavit and Chambord and stir to combine. Slowly pour in the dry white wine, stirring gently. Refrigerate for at least 2 hours or as long as overnight. (Remove the mint leaves from the sangria after 2 hours.)

When ready to serve, slowly add the sparkling wine, stirring gently with a long-handled wooden spoon. Slowly pour the sangria into champagne flutes, wineglasses, or other decorative glasses, allowing fruit pieces to fall into the glasses.

SERVES 6 TO 8

SANGRÍA DE CAVA

SPARKLING WINE SANGRIA

STEP INTO THE XAMPANYERÍA! INSPIRED BY THE WONDERFUL Champagne bars of Barcelona, which serve a variety of Cavas along with tapas. I've taken the basic sangria methodology and applied it to Spain's insatiable thirst for the bubbly. These refreshingly inventive concoctions of fresh fruit and sparkling wine move the drink beyond its place in casual entertaining to a level of high celebration.

To stay true to sangria's Spanish origins, a good Cava is the ideal sparkling wine to use, but any moderately priced brut or extra-dry sparkling wine, Prosecco, or Champagne will do fine. Light and effervescent, these wines allow fruit flavors to shine through more intensely than the more robust red wine–based sangrias.

And with the built-in carbonation, there is no need for the usual splash of club soda. Given the nature of Champagne's bubbliness, you should add it to the ingredients right before serving to preserve the bubbles.

Note: When you are ready to pour in the sparkling wine, always stir your pitcher of ingredients with a wooden or plastic spoon, as the carbonation reacts to metal and the bubbles will dissipate.

Sparkling sangrias complement a variety of dishes, such as a brunch of omelets, cheese soufflés or quiche, and fresh fruit; as well as shellfish or cold roast chicken; and a dessert of fresh berries and explorateur cheeses.

Papaya Hibiscus Sparkling Sangria

The scent of the Caribbean infuses this equatorial sangria. Fresh slices of delicately sweet-tart papaya meld perfectly with the island flavors of sour orange curaçao liqueur and tangy, citrus-like hibiscus blossoms, which also bring a deep red blush to the beverage. Dried hibiscus blossoms can be found at Latin markets, and if you are fortunate enough to come across the fresh blossoms of the Jamaican *Hibiscus sabdariffa,* by all means use them instead.

½ cup water

2 tablespoons sugar

10 dried or fresh edible hibiscus blossoms

2 cups peeled, seeded, and cubed papaya (see note)

2 lime slices

½ cup papaya nectar

3 ounces orange curaçao

750ml bottle sparkling wine, chilled

About 3 cups ice cubes (optional)

In a small saucepan, bring the water to a boil. Add the sugar, stirring slowly until dissolved. Reduce heat to low, add the hibiscus blossoms, and let simmer for 5 minutes. Remove from heat and let cool.

In a large (at least 2-quart) glass pitcher, combine the papaya cubes and lime slices. Add the papaya nectar, orange curaçao, and brewed hibiscus liquid (including the blossoms), and stir gently to combine. Refrigerate for about 2 hours.

When ready to serve, slowly add the sparkling wine, stirring gently with a long-handled wooden spoon. Fill highballs, wineglasses, or other decorative glasses with ice cubes, if using, and slowly pour the sangria over the ice, allowing fruit pieces and flowers to fall into the glasses.

Note: Look for papayas with golden yellow skin that is soft to the touch. Solo is the most common variety, but if you can find strawberry papaya from Hawaii, it is sweeter in flavor.

SERVES 4

Pink Grapefruit Sparkling Sangria

I absolutely adore the sweet-tartness of pink grapefruit, so for me this sangria defines pure, unadulterated bliss. It is sublime in its simplicity, but if you prefer a more complex flavor, the orange tones of Grand Marnier will add depth and fortification, while the rich raspberry flavor of Chambord liqueur will supply a sweeter touch.

2 small pink grapefruits, sliced

2 ounces lemonade

2 ounces Grand Marnier or Chambord (optional)

2 tablespoons sugar

750ml bottle sparkling wine, chilled

About 3 cups ice cubes (optional)

In a large (at least 2-quart) glass pitcher, combine the grapefruit slices, lemonade, liqueur (if using), and sugar. With a long-handled wooden spoon, muddle the mixture to release the fruit juices, and stir until the sugar has dissolved. Refrigerate for about 2 hours.

When ready to serve, slowly add the sparkling wine, stirring gently with a long-handled wooden spoon. Fill highballs, wineglasses, or other decorative glasses with ice cubes, if using, and slowly pour the sangria over the ice, allowing grapefruit slices to fall into the glasses.

SERVES 4

Raspberry Lemoncello Sparkling Sangria

It's summertime and the living is easy, especially when the exuberant flavors of this refreshing sangria hit you. One sip—complete with tangy raspberry and the sweet lemony kick of Lemoncello liqueur, an Italian import—will conjure up a carefree holiday in Capri.

1 cup fresh or frozen raspberries, rinsed

Zest of 1 lemon

3 ounces pink lemonade

2 ounces Lemoncello or other lemon liqueur

750ml bottle sparkling wine, chilled

About 3 cups ice cubes (optional)

In a large (at least 2-quart) glass pitcher, mix together the raspberries, lemon zest, lemonade, and Lemoncello. Refrigerate for about 2 hours.

When ready to serve, slowly add the sparkling wine, stirring gently with a long-handled wooden spoon. Fill highballs, wineglasses, or other decorative glasses with ice cubes, if using, and slowly pour the sangria over the ice, allowing raspberries to fall into the glasses.

SERVES 4

Cucumber Pimm's Sparkling Sangria

An English favorite takes an excursion into Andalusia, culminating in this light, sparkling sangria that is perfumed with English hothouse cucumbers (great choice for lack of seeds), lemon, Valencia orange, and Pimm's No.1, an herbal gin-based liqueur. An excellent choice for serving after an afternoon of power shopping.

1½ cups sliced English cucumbers

½ lemon, sliced

1 orange, sliced

4 ounces Pimm's No.1

2 ounces fresh orange juice

1 tablespoon sugar

750ml bottle sparkling wine, chilled

About 3 cups ice cubes (optional)

In a large (at least 2-quart) glass pitcher, combine the cucumber, lemon, and orange slices, Pimm's, orange juice, and sugar, and stir until the sugar has dissolved. Refrigerate for about 2 hours.

When ready to serve, slowly add the sparkling wine, stirring gently with a long-handled wooden spoon. Fill highballs, wineglasses, or other decorative glasses with ice cubes, if using, and slowly pour the sangria over the ice, allowing cucumber and citrus slices to fall into the glasses.

SERVES 4

Havana Banana Sparkling Sangria

For a delirious, sun-kissed pitcher of tropical lusciousness, this sangria blends the equatorial flavors of banana, pineapple, and mango with the warmth of rum, the zing of lime, and the indulgent effervescence of sparkling wine. This is the perfect libation for your next balmy-weather patio party.

2 cups cubed fresh or frozen pineapple

1 mango, peeled, pitted, and diced (see note)

1 ripe banana, peeled and sliced

2 tablespoons lime zest

2 ounces banana liqueur

2 ounces Triple Sec or other orange liqueur

2 ounces light rum

750ml bottle sparkling wine, chilled

About 3 cups ice cubes (optional)

In a large (at least 2-quart) glass pitcher, mix together the pineapple, mango, banana slices, and lime zest. Add the liqueurs and rum, and stir to combine. Refrigerate for about 2 hours.

When ready to serve, slowly add the sparkling wine, stirring gently with a long-handled wooden spoon. Fill highballs, wineglasses, or other decorative glasses with ice cubes, if using, and. slowly pour the sangria over the ice, allowing fruit pieces to fall into the glasses.

Note: Preparing a mango can be a messy business but well worth it. With a sharp knife, pare off the skin. Then, standing the mango on its long, narrow side, carve off the flesh lengthwise, getting as close as you can to the long, flat seed at the center. Dice the mango slices into cubes for drink preparation.

SERVES 4

Vanilla Bean Kumquat Sparkling Sangria

For an exotic libation seemingly straight from a café in Madagascar, try this heady sangria infused with fragrant vanilla bean, tart kumquat, and decadent Tuaca liqueur, perfectly matched with its tones of vanilla, herbs, and orange. The warmth of the vanilla flavors plays off the spunky tartness of the citrusy kumquats—simply lovely! If you cannot find kumquats, substitute 2 tangerines, sliced.

2 cups kumquats (approximately 20), halved and seeded

1 vanilla bean, broken into small pieces

3 ounces Tuaca

2 tablespoons sugar

750ml bottle sparkling wine, chilled

About 3 cups ice cubes (optional)

In a large (at least 2-quart) glass pitcher, combine the kumquats, vanilla bean, Tuaca, and sugar, and with a long-handled wooden spoon muddle the mixture to release the fruit juice and dissolve the sugar. Refrigerate for about 2 hours.

When ready to serve, slowly add the sparkling wine, gently stirring with a long-handled wooden spoon. Fill highballs, wineglasses, or other decorative glasses with ice cubes, if using, and slowly pour the sangria over the ice, allowing kumquat halves (but not vanilla bean pieces) to fall into the glasses.

SERVES 4

SANGRÍA ROSADA Y SANGRÍA DE MOSCATEL

ROSÉ WINE SANGRIA AND MUSCAT WINE SANGRIA

TRADITIONAL SANGRIAS ARE MADE WITH DRY, LIGHT

red wine, but for those who have a desire to venture into other exciting wine possibilities, this selection of sangrias won't disappoint. Rosé wines have a way of conjuring up visions of seductive rendezvous, no doubt induced by the blush of pink in the wine. Contrary to popular belief, there are great-tasting rosés available, such as the salmon-pink-hued fruity rosés from Provence, France, and those from Navarre, Spain, where garnacha grapes are grown for a very drinkable fruity, young rosado (Spanish rosé). Serve a pitcher of rosé sangria to accompany a plate of Manchego cheese with Medjool dates;

or Pears with Spanish Goat Cheese, Tomato, and Basil (page 75); or paella.

For those who enjoy a sweeter libation, there are two sangrias made with a blending of sweet Moscatel (Muscat) wine and brut sparkling wine—for a bit of dry to counterbalance the sweet. They satisfy the desire for a dessert wine and lighten it with effervescence. Although a Spanish Moscatel is the ideal wine to use, California produces a few great Muscat blanc wines that work quite well in these sangrias. Enjoy your Muscat sangria with an omelet, or with fresh fruit, apple strudel, or a chocolate dessert.

Lime and Roses Rosé Sangria

The sweet scent of rose petals subtly permeates this aromatic sangria, mingling with citrus tones and a pleasantly fruity rosé wine. The added effervescence of sparkling wine is purely for seductive purposes. The more beautifully fragrant the rose, the better, as I discovered with one particular batch that was nicely accented by a yellowish pink rose with a distinctly lemony scent. (Avoid those that have a too-strong perfumey or soapy smell.) This combination is also wonderful with a white wine in place of the rosé or, for special occasions and romantic rendezvous, sparkling rosé wine.

½ cup fragrant edible rose petals
  (from about 2 roses), rinsed gently

2 lime slices

2 orange slices

1 ounce Cointreau

2 ounces brandy

2 tablespoons honey, warmed

750ml bottle dry rosé wine, chilled

6 ounces sparkling wine, chilled

About 3 cups ice cubes (optional)

In a large (at least 2-quart) glass pitcher, gently mix together the rose petals and citrus slices. Add the Cointreau, brandy, and honey, and stir to combine. Slowly pour in the rosé wine, stirring gently. Refrigerate for at least 2 hours or as long as overnight.

When ready to serve, slowly add the sparkling wine, stirring gently with a long-handled wooden spoon. Fill highballs, wineglasses, or other decorative glasses with ice cubes, if using, and slowly pour the sangria over the ice, allowing rose petals and citrus slices to fall into the glasses.

SERVES 4

Three-Berry Basil Rosé Sangria

This frivolous violet-red sangria has a profusion of berries wonderfully accented by aromatic basil leaves and the honey-whisky warmth of Drambuie. It's perfect for a leisurely summer picnic, complete with a mild Spanish cheese and loaf of crusty bread.

½ cup fresh or frozen raspberries, rinsed

½ cup fresh or frozen blueberries, rinsed

½ cup fresh or frozen blackberries, rinsed

¼ cup fresh basil leaves (about 6 medium leaves)

1 ounce brandy

2 ounces Drambuie

750ml bottle dry rosé wine, chilled

12 ounces club soda, chilled

About 3 cups ice cubes

4 to 6 basil sprigs for garnish (optional)

In a large (at least 2-quart) glass pitcher, mix together the berries and basil. Add the brandy and Drambuie, and stir to combine. Slowly pour in the wine, stirring gently. Refrigerate for at least 2 hours or as long as overnight.

When ready to serve, add the club soda and stir gently with a long-handled wooden spoon. Fill highballs, wineglasses, or other decorative glasses with ice cubes and slowly pour the sangria over the ice, allowing berries to fall into the glasses. Garnish each glass with a basil sprig, if desired.

SERVES 4 TO 6

Variation: Use sparkling lemonade in place of the club soda to add a refreshing citrus flavor, or sparkling wine for a festive touch.

Saffron Mango Muscat Sangria

Elements of Arabian aromatherapy rendezvous with the Caribbean in this lush melding of pleasantly bitter saffron, refreshing lime, and bliss-inducing pineapple and mango—all blended with sweet Muscat wine and the effervescence of Cava. The floating threads of orange-red saffron make for a visually striking and festive sangria.

2 cups cubed fresh or frozen pineapple

1 mango, peeled, pitted, and sliced or cubed (see note, page 58)

1 lime, sliced

1 to 2 pinches of saffron threads

2 ounces brandy

750ml bottle Muscat wine, chilled

750ml bottle Cava or other sparkling wine, chilled

In a large (at least 2-quart) glass pitcher, mix together the pineapple, mango, and lime slices. Add the saffron and brandy, and stir to combine. Slowly pour in the Muscat wine, stirring gently. Refrigerate for at least 2 hours or as long as overnight.

When ready to serve, slowly add the sparkling wine, stirring gently with a long-handled wooden spoon to combine. Slowly pour the sangria into champagne flutes, wineglasses, or other decorative glasses, allowing fruit pieces to fall into the glasses.

SERVES 6 TO 8

Strawberry, Orange, and Muscat Grape Sparkling Sangria

If you have ever experienced the pleasure of tasting a sweet, ripe muscat grape, you will understand the motivation behind making a wine from this succulent fruit. This sangria is a veritable dessert in a glass, made with muscat grapes (if you cannot find them, omit), red and green grapes, strawberries, and orange, all infusing Muscat wine, with the addition of a bottle of bubbly for fun.

½ cup seedless green grapes, halved

½ cup seedless red grapes, halved

½ cup muscat grapes, halved (optional)

1½ cups strawberries, hulled and sliced

½ orange, sliced

2 ounces cognac

750ml bottle Muscat wine, chilled

750ml bottle sparkling wine, chilled

In a large (at least 2-quart) glass pitcher, mix together the grapes, strawberries, and orange slices. Add the cognac and stir to combine. Slowly pour in the Muscat wine, stirring gently. Refrigerate for at least 2 hours or as long as overnight.

When ready to serve, slowly add the sparkling wine, stirring gently with a long-handled wooden spoon. Slowly pour the sangria into champagne flutes, wineglasses, or other decorative glasses, allowing fruit pieces to fall into the glasses.

SERVES 6 TO 8

SPANISH TAPAS

IN SPAIN, "TAPAS-HOPPING" FROM WINE BAR TO WINE BAR goes back centuries to traveling the ancient dusty roads of the southern Andalusian region. As a way to lure travelers, roadside Inns and taverns would offer a slice of bread and ham along with the ordered glass of wine. The term tapas—meaning "to cover"—came about literally, as these open sandwiches served as a great way to keep the road dust and fruit flies out of the wine, at the same time providing a bit of sustenance to buffer the alcohol. As competition heated up among wine bars, motivating culinary creativity, this small morsel evolved into increasingly more elaborate regional specialties.

Today, this revered national pastime revs up around dusk and reflects the spirit and soul of social life in any given town in Spain. People meet up with friends at a favorite tapas bar and then, as the evening unfolds, make a pilgrimage from one bar to the next, savoring the various house specialties along with a fino sherry, a glass of wine from the local bodega, or the house sangria.

In the Andalusian spirit of the social appetizer, here are small delicacies that allow an easy flow of conversation and are the perfect balance of salty and savory to the light and fruity sweetness of a refreshing pitcher of sangria. This selection of authentic Spanish tapas contains regional favorites, such as the Moorish-influenced Grilled Garlic Shrimp with Saffron (page 71), and zesty marinated olives, along with a few exciting variations, such as Pears with Spanish Goat Cheese, Tomato, and Basil (page 75).

Grilled Garlic Shrimp with Saffron

The Moorish influence is prevalent in Spanish Mediterranean cuisine. Saffron—a spice with a powerful aroma and deep red-orange color—is one of the treasured contributions. Be careful cooking with it, as a little goes a long way! Flavored with a saffron-garlic marinade, this grilled shrimp is the perfect summer accompaniment to a white wine or sparkling sangria. Try it with the Sangri-la (page 37) or Pink Grapefruit Sparkling Sangria (page 52).

⅓ cup extra-virgin olive oil

2 pinches of saffron threads

2 tablespoons fresh lime juice

2 garlic cloves, finely minced

20 raw jumbo shrimp, peeled and deveined

In a medium nonreactive bowl, whisk together the olive oil, saffron, lime juice, and garlic. Add the shrimp and toss to coat. Cover and refrigerate for 2 hours.

Prepare a fire in a grill to medium-high heat.

Push shrimp onto 4 metal skewers, allowing the excess marinade to drain off. Grill until just opaque in the center, about 2 minutes per side.

To serve, place each skewer on an individual small plate.

SERVES 4

Grilled Asparagus with Almonds

Fresh grilled asparagus is a spring and summer pleasure not to be missed, and it is made even more pleasurable with the Spanish-Arabian element of rich, roasted almonds. For best grilling results, try to find very thin asparagus spears and cook them over an ebbing fire, to add a subtle grilled flavor. This dish pairs beautifully with the Mango Lemongrass Sangria (page 48) or Tangerine, Watermelon, and Grapefruit Sangria (page 38).

1 tablespoon butter

¼ cup sliced almonds

1¼ pounds fresh asparagus, trimmed

¼ cup extra-virgin olive oil

1 garlic clove, minced

Prepare a fire in a grill, and let coals burn down to medium heat.

Meanwhile, in a small sauté pan melt the butter over medium heat. Add the almonds and sauté until light brown. Set aside.

In a large bowl, toss the asparagus with the olive oil and garlic. Grill over medium to low coals, turning the spears as needed until they are tender, about 6 minutes. Use a vegetable-grilling basket if the spears are likely to fall through your grill. (Cover the grill if necessary to maintain the heat.)

Remove from the grill and transfer to a serving plate. Top with the almond-butter mixture, toss, and serve.

SERVES 6

Pears with Spanish Goat Cheese, Tomato, and Basil

Here is a decadent and aromatic summer *ensalada* of ripe Bosc pears, tangy goat cheese, sweet cherry tomatoes, and basil—it just doesn't get any better than this! Look for "drunken" Spanish goat cheese, which is wine-cured and has a smooth, delicately sharp taste and velvety purple rind (dyed from the curing process). If you cannot find it, substitute another goat cheese or the more mellow buffalo mozzarella. As an accompaniment, serve the Summer Melon Sangria (page 46) or Roman Holiday sangria (page 40).

2 ripe Bosc (or other) pears, cored
  and sliced ¼ inch thick

12 basil leaves

6 ounces Spanish goat cheese, thinly
  sliced (see headnote)

10 small orange or regular cherry
  tomatoes, halved

¼ cup sherry vinaigrette (recipe follows)

1¼ teaspoons ground cinnamon
  for dusting

On a serving plate, arrange the pear slices, basil leaves, and cheese slices, alternating them. Distribute the cherry tomatoes on top. Slowly drizzle the vinaigrette over the top. Dust with the cinnamon and serve immediately.

SERVES 4 TO 6

SHERRY VINAIGRETTE

½ cup extra-virgin olive oil

¼ cup balsamic vinegar

¼ cup fino sherry (see note)

In a small bowl, whisk together the olive oil, balsamic vinegar, and sherry until well combined.

   Note: If you prefer a sweeter vinaigrette, an oloroso, a sweeter sherry, can be used.

MAKES 1 CUP

Citrus Zest Olives

Olives from the Spanish Mediterranean are abundant and varied, which is not surprising, given that Spain's olive plantations are some of the largest in the world. These fruits grown from gnarled and ancient trees range from the famed Savilles, which are sweet, to the meaty manzanillas to gordales—prune-sized, home-cured olives. Many specialty markets in North America now offer an "olive bar" with a selection of olives, some seasoned, some merely cured. For this recipe, look for either manzanilla olives in a light marinade of olive oil and brine or montequilla de murcia olives, as they are preferable to canned varieties. This marinade subtly infuses the olives with just the right amount of citrusy zing. Serve with the Stone Fruit Zurra (page 25) or the Spanish Harlem Sangria (page 21).

2 cups manzanilla, montequilla de murcia, or other green olives

½ cup extra-virgin olive oil

½ cup balsamic vinegar

2 tablespoons orange zest

2 tablespoons lime zest

1 tablespoon black peppercorns

Drain the olives, if necessary, and discard any olive brine. Place the olives in a medium bowl together with the rest of the ingredients. With a wooden spoon, stir the olives in the marinade, turning to coat them. Cover the bowl and refrigerate for at least 3 days before serving. The olives will keep for up to 3 weeks.

MAKES 2 CUPS

Classic Andalusian Gazpacho

This recipe is in the classic Andalusian style. Although a multitude of chilled gazpacho soup variations can be found throughout Spain, one key element remains constant: using the freshest, ripest tomatoes in season. Gazpacho goes well with both light red wine and white wine sangrias.

2 to 3 inches baguette or rustic white bread, crust removed

½ cup water

2 large garlic cloves

2 teaspoons sea salt

¼ cup sherry vinegar

½ cup light extra-virgin olive oil

1 teaspoon sugar

½ teaspoon ground cumin

1 shallot, finely chopped

1 red bell pepper, stemmed, seeded, and diced

1 yellow bell pepper, stemmed, seeded, and diced

½ cucumber, peeled, seeded, and diced

4 large ripe tomatoes, cored and quartered

Freshly ground pepper to taste

GARNISHES:
1 small cucumber, peeled, seeded, and finely chopped

1 small green plus 1 small red bell pepper, stemmed, seeded, and finely chopped

1 small onion, finely chopped

Soak the bread in the ½ cup water for 1 minute, then squeeze dry and discard the water.

With a large knife, finely mince and mash the garlic with the salt. Place the garlic, bread, vinegar, olive oil, sugar, and cumin in a blender, and combine to produce a thick sauce. Transfer to a large bowl.

Place the shallot, bell peppers, cucumber, and tomatoes in the blender and blend until smooth. Pour into the bowl containing the bread mixture and stir until well combined. Cover and refrigerate for at least 4 hours or up to 48 hours. Serve cold in chilled individual soup bowls and top with pepper. Serve the garnishes in smaller bowls.

SERVES 4

INDEX

TABLE OF EQUIVALENTS

The exact equivalents in the following tables have been rounded for convenience.

LIQUID/DRY MEASURES

U.S.	METRIC
¼ teaspoon	1.25 milliliters
½ teaspoon	2.5 milliliters
1 teaspoon	5 milliliters
1 tablespoon (3 teaspoons)	15 milliliters
1 fluid ounce (2 tablespoons)	30 milliliters
¼ cup	60 milliliters
⅓ cup	80 milliliters
½ cup	120 milliliters
1 cup	240 milliliters
1 pint (2 cups)	480 milliliters
1 quart (4 cups, 32 ounces)	960 milliliters
1 gallon (4 quarts)	3.84 liters
1 ounce (by weight)	28 grams
1 pound	454 grams
2.2 pounds	1 kilogram

1 medium lemon = 3 tablespoons juice

1 medium lime = 2 tablespoons juice

1 medium orange = ⅓ cup juice

OVEN TEMPERATURE

FAHRENHEIT	CELSIUS	GAS
250	120	½
275	140	1
300	150	2
325	160	3
350	180	4
375	190	5
400	200	6
425	220	7
450	230	8
475	240	9
500	260	10

LENGTH

U.S.	METRIC
⅛ inch	3 millimeters
¼ inch	6 millimeters
½ inch	12 millimeters
1 inch	2.5 centimeters